# BOOK OF SPELLS
## SPELLS, RITUALS, AND RECIPES

© MILLA WALSH

# Blessing and Protection Spells

# Love and Relationship Spells

# Household Spells

# Banishing Spells

# Magical Powders

# Bottle Spells

# Ritual Baths

# Chants

# Basic Oils

# To Bless a Person

<u>You will need the following</u>:

White candle
Figurine of the same sex as the person whom the blessing is for
Myrrh, rosemary, or clove oil

<u>Instructions</u>:

Dress the candle.

After lighting the candle say the following:

*(Name) may you be blessed*
*May all good things come to you*
*And no harm come to you*
*(If you have anything specific you wish for this person, such as finding a job,*
*insert it here beginning with the words "May you")*

Extinguish the candle by pinching it out only. Repeat this process for a total of 7 days. The candle should finish on the 7th day.

# To Bless a House

You will need the following:

Cleaning supplies to clean wood work, wood floors, and/or carpet: mop, cleaning fluid, bucket, rags, or a vacuum.
Brand new broom
Sage smudge stick
Salt
Blessed water

Instructions:

Begin by vacuuming if there is carpet, then proceed to the wood floors, and last do the baseboards.

When finished, take the dirty water and throw it into the front yard. If there is no front yard, walk with the water to the nearest intersection and discard it toward the east.

Back inside the home, light the smudge stick and go through every room in the house, wafting the smoke up, down, and into corners. You may recite a prayer of your choice.

When the smudge stick is finished, take the new broom and begin sweeping from the back of the house towards the front. When you are done, sweep out the front door. If there is no dirt left in the house, sweep anyway.

Take the blessed water to every entry point in the house, doors and windows. Sprinkle a bit of water at each point. While sprinkling at each location, say the following:

*May only good spirits and peaceful people enter here*

Last, sprinkle salt at each of the four corners of the house.

# To Bless a Depressed Person

You will need the following:

White candle
Needle
Red cloth bag
3 cloves
Dried sage leaf
Small rose quartz

Instructions:

Carve the name of the person you are blessing into the candle.

Light the candle, focusing your mind on the person.

When you feel ready, place the cloves, sage, and rose quartz into the bag and close it.

Pass the closed bag through the flame of the candle 3 times.

Place the bag to the left of the candle and wait for the candle to finish. During this time, you may think silently or speak out loud your wishes and prayers for the depressed person.

When the candle is finished, give the bag to the person and request they keep with them for at least 7 days.

# For Good Health

You will need the following:

Glass of apple juice
Cinnamon stick
White candle

Instructions:

Light the candle.

Stir the apple juice around with the cinnamon stick and leave the cinnamon in the juice.

Drink a few sips and say:

*Goddess bless body and soul*
*Health and wellness is my goal*

Repeat until the juice is gone.

This ritual can be repeated daily.

# Healing Witch's Ladder

<u>You will need the following</u>:

Blue cord or ribbon at least 24" in length
Gray feather
Garlic clove
Fresh rosemary
4 additional items relating to the person to be healed

<u>Instructions</u>:

Tie each item, in any order, with equal space between them, on the blue cord. This is the ladder. This should be hung high off the ground, vertically, in the home of the person to be healed until they are better.

# To Clear Obstacles From Your Path

You will need the following:

Purple candle
Rosemary oil
White parchment & blessed pen
Fireproof dish

Instructions:

Begin by visualizing any specific obstacles.  Also include general obstacles.  Proceed only once you have clearly have visualized these.

Anoint the candle.

Write on the piece of parchment "All blocks are now removed."

Fold the paper three times.

Light the candle and say:

*Fire drakes, please aid me in my quest*
*turn back any negativity being sent*

Repeat this 3 times.  On the 3rd repetition, burn the folded paper and place it in your fireproof dish.

Once the paper is reduced to ash, pinch your candle out.

# Ritual Cleanse for Body and Spirit

You will need the following:

2 white candles
Holy or blessed water
Copy of Psalm 37, unless memorized

Wash cloth

Instructions:

This ritual works best in the nude.

Place a candle on each side of your body and light them.

While standing or sitting, soak the cloth in the blessed or holy water and wipe down your entire body.

Recite Psalm 37 in a low voice.

When finished, air dry only, and dispose of the holy water into earth.

# To Bless a Person with Kindness

You will need the following:

Small glass jar
Honey
White parchment & blessed pen
White or silver candle
Full moon

Instructions:

This spell should be completed in full moonlight.

Fill the glass jar with honey.

Write the name of the person you are blessing with kindness on the parchment.

Fold the parchment into quarters and place it in the jar, then seal the jar.

Light your candle and spend a few minutes visualizing the person you are blessing. Once you have visualized them, begin to attribute to their personality kindness in any way you choose. This could be kind words, kind deeds, whatever you see.

After visualizing, drip wax around the jar lid to seal it.

Leave the jar outside overnight to absorb the moon's energy.

The next morning, retrieve the jar and place it on your altar or another special place where it is visible.

This spell is good for a lunar cycle. When the lunar cycle has completed, if the spell is to be done again, bury the original jar and start over.

# To Bury Troubles or Strife Between Two People

You will need the following:

Both people involved
Perennial plant of the caster's choice
Appropriate gardening tools

Instructions:

Everyone must gather outside in the location where the plant is to be placed.

The two people must agree to work together and dig a hole to place the plant.

Once the hole is dug, the two people should sit down cross-legged, facing each other, with the hole in between them.

The caster should remove a strand of hair from each person, and place it in the hole.

Both people should hold both hands, wrists crossed, above the hole.

Both people and the caster should close their eyes and visualize peace and harmony.

When this is done, the caster should request both people say, simultaneously, "*I'm sorry.*"

Both people should place their hands on the plant, lower it into the ground, and fill in the dirt.

Once this is complete, there is no need to repeat the spell. This spell should never be discussed by anyone out loud. If in the future, any troubles arise, the two people should visit their plant together and sit in peace.

# To Protect a Person from Nightmares

You will need the following:

Broomcorn
Rosemary
Salt

Instructions:

Sprinkle salt in the four corners of the room where the person affected by nightmares sleeps regularly.

The rosemary and broomcorn should be placed under their pillow for the night.

The next day, the broomcorn and rosemary should be scattered at any crossroads. This will take all evil spirits and negativity and remove it from the area and person.

This ritual can be completed weekly.

# Safe Travel Charm

You will need the following:

Small red cloth bag
Dirt from your yard
Chunks of rock salt
Small piece of real silver

Instructions:

If you don't have a yard, you should try and get dirt from a family's yard or as close to your home as possible.

Put everything in the bag and carry it with you as you travel. It should be buried in the same place as the dirt originally came from when the journey is over.

# Talisman to Protect on a Journey

<u>You will need the following</u>:

Needle & white thread
Blue cloth
Comfrey root

<u>Instructions</u>:

Place the comfrey root on the cloth and fold in half.

Sew the sides of the cloth together so the comfrey root is sewn in tight. While sewing, visualize the person who will carry the bag as walking down a safe path with a white light of protection surrounding them.

When finished, the person taking the journey should carry the bag for the duration of travel time.

Upon safe return, the bag should be opened and the root discarded into that person's yard.

# To Protect From an Enemy

<u>You will need the following</u>:

Black candle
3 pieces of white cord at least 6" in length each

<u>Instructions</u>:

Light the candle.

Tie the first cord around the bottom of the candle and say:

*By three and nine, your power I bind*
*By the moon and sun, my will be done*

Tie the second cord around the middle of the candle and say:

*Sky and sea, keep harm from me*
*Cord go round, power be bound*

Tie the third cord around the top of the candle (stay a safe distance under the flame) and say:

*Light revealed, this spell is sealed*
*So I will it, so mote it be*

Snuff out the candle to finish.

# To Bless the Marriage Bed

<u>You will need the following</u>:

Pink cord 24″ in length
Ylang ylang oil

<u>Instructions</u>:

Put a couple drops of oil on each hand and anoint the cord.

Start at one end of the cord and tie a knot while saying:

*With knot of one, this is where love comes*

Tie the second knot while saying:

*With knot of two, this love stays true*

Tie the third knot while saying:

*With knot of three, so mote it be*

This cord should be draped or laid (not tied) somewhere on the bed, like across the headboard or around a bed post.

This spell can be refreshed annually.

# To Make a Wish

You will need the following:

Lavender candle
Lavender oil
7 pieces of parchment & blessed pen

Instructions:

Anoint the candle and light it.

On parchment, write out your wish, speak your wish out loud, and burn the parchment.

Snuff out the candle.

Do this again for 6 more days to complete the spell.

# Threshold Protection

<u>You will need the following</u>:

Handful of salt
Teaspoon of garlic powder

<u>Instructions</u>:

Stir ingredients together and dust them over the threshold you want to protect. This will protect from negative energy and can be refreshed weekly.

# Blessed Water

You will need the following:

Water

Instructions:

While holding the water, say:

*O great Goddess and God, I call upon you*
*I am in need of your help*
*Bless this water with your power and purification*
*Bless this water with your wisdom and strength*
*With water so blessed, this will harm none*
*So I will it, so mote it be*

# To Bless a Book of Shadows

Blue candle
White candle
Red candle
Green candle
Compass
Book of Shadows

Instructions:

Put the green candle to the North, the white candle to the East, the blue candle to the West, and the red candle to the South. The Book of Shadows should lie in the center.

Light the green candle and say:

*Bless this book with the power of the Earth*

Light the red candle and say:

*Bless this book with the power of Fire*

Light the blue candle and say:

*Bless this book with the power of Water*

Light the white candle and say:

*Bless this book with the power of Air*

Leave the book in place until the candles have finished.

# To Bless a Book of Shadows II

You will need the following:

White candle
Blessed pen
Book of Shadows
Midnight

Instructions:

Begin at midnight by lighting the candle.

By candlelight only, write the following in the front of the Book of Shadows:

"Goddess please protect this book from wandering eyes and prying looks, fill it with your ancient powers at this the witching hour."

You can also read the passage out loud after it has been written.

Snuff out the candle when you are ready.

# Love Letter to Right a Wrong

<u>You will need the following</u>:

Parchment & blessed pen with red ink
Scent that symbolizes yourself
5 red rose petals
Red candle

<u>Instructions</u>:

Light the candle.

Sincerely write out on the parchment what you have done, and why you know it was wrong.

When satisfied, add in 5 reasons you love and appreciate the person you have wronged.

With the parchment flat, add your scent to it and also the rose petals.

Fold 3 times, and insert into the envelope.

Close the envelope and seal with wax. It is important to deliver this letter to the person you have wronged as soon as possible, and you must personally deliver it.

# To Draw a Friend

<u>You will need the following</u>:

Large candle in the color of your choice
Needle
Parchment & blessed pen
Jar
Salt

<u>Instructions</u>:

Write down your strongest personality traits on the parchment and fold it 3 times.

Carve those same traits into the candle.

Add the salt and the parchment to the jar.

Light your candle and seal the jar with wax.

Place the jar and the candle in your bedroom, near the bed, in a safe place.

Each night before you go to sleep, light the candle for 5 minutes.

You can either look at the jar, or hold the jar, and spend this 5 minutes meditating on finding a wonderful friend.  Picture the smoke from your candle entering the air of your room, then your house, then out into the world, looking for your friend.

You have to be somewhere to be seen, so be out and be looking.  When the person you are seeking is around, you should be drawn to them.

# Silver Ring to Attract a Mate

You will need the following:

New silver ring
White cloth
White wine
Full moon
Small spade or shovel

Instructions:

Outside under the full moon, look up and say:

*Blessed Goddess fair and true*
*This silver gift I offer you*
*Bless this ring and make it shine*
*Bring a lover to be mine*

Dig a small hole, wrap the ring in cloth, and cover it over.

Anoint the ground with white wine.

Leave the ring buried for a full lunar cycle.

When the appropriate time has passed, dig up the ring, and wear it to attract a new love in your life.

# To Draw a Lover

You will need the following:

Access to ocean
Parchment & blessed pen
Full moon

Instructions:

Under the light of full moon, find a small seashell. You will be attracted to the seashell and that is how you will know it is the right one.

While holding the shell, visualize the traits you would like to see in a potential mate.

Once visualized, write down the traits on your parchment and then fold the paper 3 times.

Place the paper in the shell, and the shell in shallow water.

As the tide comes in your shell and parchment will be drawn out into the ocean. This will set in motion the tides to bring forth your mate.

# To Draw a Lover II

You will need the following:

Red candle
Carnelian
Jasmine incense
Clear weather

Instructions:

On any night where the stars are visible, assemble your ingredients at an open window.

Light the candle and incense.

Take the carnelian to the window and hold it up toward the brightest star you can see, then say:

*Star of my love*
*Burn so bright*
*Unite my true love to me*
*So I will it, so mote it be*

Place the carnelian back with the candle and incense, allowing both to finish. Keep the carnelian either on your altar or on your windowsill until you have found your mate.

# To Enhance Love in a Relationship

You will need the following:

White candle
Needle
3 thorns from a white rose bush

Instructions:

Carve into the candle "All my love return to me" 3 times.

Place the 3 thorns on the left side of candle.

Light the candle.

Spend 5 minutes visualizing yourself sending out all the love you are capable of sending towards your target. Don't focus on their love for you, just on your love for them.

After at least 5 minutes, snuff out the candle.

Repeat this spell daily until the candle is burned down completely.

When the candle is finished, keep the 3 thorns under your bed indefinitely.

# To Attract New Love

You will need the following:

2 lodestones
Magnetic sand
Red candle
2 white parchments & blessed pen with red ink
Altar

Instructions:

Place the lodestones a few inches apart, with the candle in between but slightly behind them.

Place the magnetic sand in between the lodestones but slightly in front of them.

Write your name 3 times on one parchment, and write "My Lover" on the other parchment 3 times.

Fold each parchment in half. The parchment with your name, place under the lodestone on the left. The parchment that says "My Lover" should be placed under the lodestone on the right.

Light the candle.

Sprinkle 1/7 of the magnetic sand on the 2 lodestones.

For at least 3 minutes, visualize yourself finding a new lover and having a wonderful and peaceful relationship, then snuff the candle.

After you have visualized, move the lodestones slightly closer together.

For the following 6 days, repeat lighting the candle, adding more magnetic sand to each lodestone, and moving them closer together.

On the 7th day, the lodestones should be covered in all of the magnetic sand, should be touching each other, and your candle should finish.

Leave the lodestones on your altar until you have attracted a new lover into your life.

# To Maintain Long Distance Love

You will need the following:

2 red cloth bags
2 rose quartz
2 sprigs of rosemary
Both people in love

Instructions:

Divide the ingredients between the 2 people.

Each person holds the red cloth bag in their left hand, and with their right hand, adds the rose quartz while saying:

*Our love will remain strong*

Each person then adds the rosemary sprigs while saying:

*Our love will remain true*

Each person then closes the bag while saying:

*No matter the time or the distance*

Now the people exchange bags, so that each person ends up with the bag their lover put together, while saying:

*So I will it, so mote it be*

The bags are to be carried by each person for the entire time they remain separated.

Once the people are reunited, they must bury the bags together to finish the spell.

# To Strengthen a Current Relationship

You will need the following:

Red apple
Honey
Strands of your hair
Strands of the other person's hair
Red cord or yarn 12" in length

Instructions:

Cut the apple in half so you can see the center seeds.

Cover both open halves of apple with honey.

Twist the strands of hair together and put them in the honey.

Using the red cord, tie the apple back together.

This should be buried on your own property, as close to your bedroom window as possible and left in place indefinitely.

# Couple's Love Spell

You will need the following:

1 picture of each person
Red candle
Blessed pen with red ink

Instructions:

Together, the couple should light and hold the candle.

Drip wax over the front of both photos, then place them together.

On the back of the other person's photo, each person should write "I love you."

The bound photos should be stored under the mattress of the bed where the couple sleeps.

# Herbal Love Box

<u>You will need the following</u>:

Small box or bowl with lid
Small quartz
Red rose petals you picked yourself
Vanilla bean
Several lavender flowers you picked yourself
Pinch of ground cinnamon or 1 cinnamon stick
White parchment & blessed pen

<u>Instructions</u>:

Combine everything in the box or bowl except the parchment, stirring together with your finger.

On the parchment, write down 5 things you are thankful for in your relationship.

Fold the paper 3 times and add it to the box.

This box should be kept in the center room of the house. It should remain untouched except for yourself and your lover.

The ingredients in the box and the parchment can be refreshed every 3 months.

# To Increase Dream Energy

You will need the following:

Small cloth bag in the color of your choice
3 apple seeds from an apple you ate yourself
Dried sage leaf
Petals of a white flower

Instructions:

Place all items in your cloth bag and sleep with it under your pillow.

The bag should be emptied and its contents replaced monthly to continue to enhance your dreams.

# To Decrease Dream Energy

You will need the following:

Clear glass
Water

Instructions:

Before bed, fill the glass with water and place it near the bed, then sleep as you normally would.

First thing upon rising, take the glass of water to the bathroom and pour it into the toilet with your left hand.

As you are pouring, visualize a sleeping peaceful body, a body that is free of intense dreams.

Flush the toilet, taking all the intensity away from you.

This ritual can be completed monthly.

# Peaceful Sleep Sachet

You will need the following:

Small cloth bag
10 whole cardamom pods
15 whole cloves
½ ounce dried mint
½ ounce dried rosemary
½ ounce salt
White candle
Pink candle
Silver candle

Instructions:

Assemble the ingredients wherever you will be working on the sachet. It should be peaceful and you should be free of interruptions while you work.

Light all the candles, placement does not matter.

Place everything in the cloth bag and seal it, while repeating:

*Sleep, dream, peace*
*Peace, sleep, dream*
*Dream, peace, sleep*

The sachet should be keep near the bed, either on a nightstand, under a pillow, or around a bedpost.

The sachet can be refreshed every 3 months.

# To Make a Wish Come True

You will need the following:

Small red flannel bag
7 Jobs Tears

Instructions:

The 7 Jobs Tears should be placed in the bag and carried on your person.

Once a day in a quiet moment, touch the bag and meditate for 1 minute on your wish.

This practice should be continued until your wish has been fulfilled, but it must be a realistic wish.

# To Increase Sexual Energy

:

Image of hummingbird

Instructions:

Select your hummingbird carefully. This could be anything: an oil painting, a ceramic figurine, or an image printed off the internet. It could even be a photograph you took yourself. The most important thing is that you are attracted to it.

Place the hummingbird on the northern wall of your bedroom. As long it remains there, your sexual energy will remain charged.

# To Enhance Romance

<u>You will need the following</u>:

Rose quartz
Small silver bowl
Handful of pink rose petals
New moon

<u>Instructions</u>:

Assemble your ingredients in the light of the new moon.

Kiss your crystal and place it in the bowl.

Sprinkle the petals in the bowl.

Place the bowl in a window that receives moonlight for 7 days.

At the end of 7 days, take the rose quartz and carry it on your person.

At the end of the lunar cycle, take the silver bowl and petals outside, and sprinkle the rose petals to the wind.

Continue to carry the rose quartz to attract romance.

# To Decrease Your Anger

You will need the following:

Teacup and saucer
Water
Spoonful of honey
Several spoonfuls of mint leaves

Instructions:

Heat the water to just boiling and pour it into your teacup over the mint leaves and honey.

Inhale the aroma while the tea steeps, focusing on your anger evaporating with the steam.

When cool enough, drink the tea slowly while mentally repeating:

*Cool my mind, leaves of mint*
*Honey, please sweeten my intent*
*For my attitude to change*
*I must send anger out of my range*

# To Overcome a Bad Habit

You will need the following:

Black candle
Clove oil
Needle
Small piece of onyx

Instructions:

Carve the bad habit into the candle.

Anoint the candle.

Light the candle and say:

*Unwanted habit, please be gone*
*Leave me when the candle is done*
*Candle burn to remove all ill*
*By the power of my will*
*So mote it be*

Allow the candle to finish. The onyx is to carry on your person, to remind you to be strong. This spell can be repeated daily if necessary, using the same onyx piece each time.

# To Make a Tough Decision

You will need the following:

Small bowl
Rocks or shells gathered from the edge of water, enough to fill the bowl
Stick taller than the bowl
Parchment & blessed pen

Instructions:

Fill the bowl with rocks or shells and place the stick in the center, pointing upwards.  There should be enough rocks or shells to hold the stick in place, and the point of the stick should rise above the rim the bowl.

Write down a summary of what you have to decide, as well as your possible choices.

Place your hand on top of the stick and say:

*To reach within me*
*To take a side*
*To use this knowledge*
*To decide*

Now close your eyes and mentally list your options.  The first option that comes to mind is the one you want to choose.

# Black Opal Charm

<u>You will need the following</u>:

Black opal

<u>Instructions</u>:

While holding the black opal in your dominant hand, say:

*This black opal of burning fire*
*Shall be imbued with the power required*
*To make my magic meet its mark*
*By the light of day or the night of dark*
*As I will it, so mote it be*

Repeat at least 3 times.

The opal should be kept on your altar as a powerful charm to aid your magic.

# Basic Reversing Spell

You will need the following:

Double action candle, red on top, black on bottom
Rue oil
Parchment & blessed pen with red ink

Instructions:

Anoint your candle and light it.

Write out what you want to reverse on the parchment and place it under the candle.

Let the candle burn for 10 minutes and snuff it out.

Repeat this for 2 additional days.

On the last day, allow the candle to finish. Take any wax remnants and carry them far from your home to dispose of them.

# Reverse Negative Energy

<u>You will need the following</u>:

Cup of salt
Lemon
Bowl
Knife

<u>Instructions</u>:

Pour the salt into the bowl and place it in the center of your altar.

Cut the lemon into 4 equal parts, place them around the bowl, and say:

*All spells against me congregate in this lemon*
*Sour spell to sour fruit*
*You must go there because it's your suit*
*All in this lemon, now I see*
*I bind you here, with your own negativity*
*And as I will it, so mote it be*

Now start sprinkling the salt on the lemon while saying:

*Uncrossed*
*This salt breaks up any attacking energy*
*As lemon dries in salt and air*
*I'm freed from harm and all despair*
*I will live happily*
*As I will it, so mote it be*

Leave the lemon on your altar. For the next few days, check to see if the lemon is drying out, or mildewing. If it dries out, the spell is complete. If it mildewed, the spell should be repeated with a fresh lemon.

# Reverse a Spell Cast Against You

You will need the following:

Hand mirror
Bell
Black string
Black candle

Instructions:

Ring the bell in each of the 4 corners of the room you are casting from.

Light your candle.

Hold the mirror behind the candle and say:

*As the mirror reflects back the light of the candle*
*So shall any negativity be reflected away from me*
*And as the mirror neither adds nor subtracts*
*Nothing shall be added or subtracted to anything reflected away from me*

Tie 3 knots into the black string and say, with each knot:

*With this string I bind this spell*
*As I will it, so mote it be*

The string should be kept indefinitely.

# Reverse a Hex Cast Against You

<u>You will need the following</u>:

Purple candle
Rosemary oil
Parchment & blessed pen
Fireproof dish

<u>Instructions</u>:

Anoint the candle and light it.

Write on the piece of paper "All hexes are removed."

Fold the paper 3 times and burn it while saying:

*Fire drakes and salamanders, aid me in my quest*
*Protect me from all forms of evil, and any negativity being sent*
*As I will it, so mote it be*

# Reverse a Simple Spell You Cast

<u>You will need the following</u>:

Magenta candle

<u>Instructions</u>:

Light the candle and repeat 3 times:

*Reverse the (be specific on the spell) magic which I cast*
*Let it not be a part of the past*
*As I will it, so mote it be*

The candle should be allowed to finish.

# Reverse a Love Spell You Cast

<u>You will need the following</u>:

White cord at least 12″ in length
Red candle

<u>Instructions</u>:

Light the candle.

Hold the white cord, tie a knot near the top, and say:

*This is the spell I cast to gain that which was not freely given*

Concentrate on the original love spell.

Do this 3 times, so that you have 3 knots.

Now start at the bottom, and going back up, untie the knot and say:

*As the knot is untied the spell is undone*
*Be free to love or not as you will*

Do this 3 times, so that you have untied all the knots.

Burn the untied cord in the candle.

# Money Talisman

Green cloth bag
Pinch of basil
3 silver coins (real silver)
Gold thread

Instructions:

Place the basil and coins in the cloth bag and bind it shut with the gold thread.

This bag should be carried with you, indefinitely, to draw wealth. When not being carried, it can be kept on your desk, or wherever it is that you pay bills.

# To Pay an Unexpected Bill

<u>You will need the following</u>:

Green candle
Cinnamon oil
Parchment & blessed pen

<u>Instructions</u>:

On the parchment, draw a representation of the bill you need to pay. You can include logos, words and dollar amounts.

Anoint the candle and light it, the parchment should be placed underneath the candle.

Take a few minutes to visualize this bill, the need to pay it, and see yourself having enough money to pay for it. Then say:

*The candle burns and lights the way*
*For the money for the bill I will pay*

Now remove the parchment and burn it, collecting the ash to throw outside your front door.

# Tonka Bean Token

You will need the following:

Tonka bean

Instructions:

Hold the Tonka bean in your hand and say:

*I have a Tonka bean*
*Because times are so lean*
*May it draw me money*
*Like bees are drawn to honey*

The Tonka bean can be kept on your altar indefinitely.

# To Get a Job

<u>You will need the following</u>:

Green candle
Photo of yourself
Dollar bill
Patchouli oil
Paperclip

<u>Instructions</u>:

Anoint the candle and then light it.

Hold the dollar bill in your hands while visualizing all the opportunities this job offers.

Once you have visualized, hold the dollar bill close enough to get warm but not singed or burned.

While the dollar bill is still warm, fold it in quarters and paperclip it to your photo.

Carry this in your pocket while on the job interview.

# Money Magnet

You will need the following:

Silver bowl
Pinch of dill
Cinnamon stick
Pine oil
Malachite

Instructions:

Add the dill and cinnamon stick to the silver bowl.

Add the pine oil, and stir with your finger.

Place the malachite in the bowl, covering it with the herbal mixture.

Leave this in place, preferably on your altar, for 7 days.

After 7 days, remove the malachite and carry it in your pocket or purse.

The silver bowl and herbs should be left in place until you have drawn money.

# Attract Prosperity to Your Home

<u>You will need the following</u>:

Brand new welcome mat
Sandalwood chips
Dried basil leaves
Silver coin

<u>Instructions</u>:

Place the mat in front of the door you and your family use most often to enter and leave the house.

Lift the doormat and underneath it sprinkle the sandalwood and basil, with the coin in the center.

Now stand directly on top of the mat, and facing away from your house, say:

*I welcome wealth into my home*
*Please stop here, there is no need to roam*
*My welcome mat is here you see*
*Bring in new prosperity*

This spell can be refreshed annually.

# Increase Your Income

<u>You will need the following</u>:

Full moon
Bowl
Blessed water
Basil

<u>Instructions</u>:

In the full moonlight, fill your bowl with blessed water and add the basil.

Stir with a finger and say:

*By the light of the moon*
*Bless me soon*
*Water and silver shine*
*Wealth is mine*

Leave the bowl in place overnight.  The following day, discard the water at the end of your driveway or sidewalk.

# Houseplant to Help Money Grow

You will need the following:

Healthy houseplant
Pinch of patchouli
Coin

Instructions:

Lay the coin on the dirt around the plant, but don't bury it.

Sprinkle the patchouli over the plant.

Take care of the plant as needed and each time you are tending the plant focus on your finances being as well cared for and as abundant as the plant.

When you receive unexpected money, spend the coin currently in the plant and replace it with a new one to keep the spell alive.

# Money Charm for Household Wealth

You will need the following:

Green cord at least 24" in length
Pine oil
Dollar bill

Instructions:

Anoint the cord with pine oil.

Begin at one end, tie a knot, and say:

*With knot of one, this spell's begun*

Tie the second knot and say:

*With knot of two, I make it true*

Tie the third knot and say:

*With knot of three, I see prosperity*

Tie the fourth knot and say:

*With knot of four, I see even more*

Tie the fifth knot and say:

*With knot of five, the spell is alive*

Roll your dollar bill into a tube and tie the cord around it. This should be stored in the highest safe place in your kitchen.

# For a Peaceful Home

<u>You will need the following</u>:

Blue cloth bag
Hairs from each member of the household
Lavender flowers
Chamomile flowers
Blue thread

<u>Instructions</u>:

Place the flowers in the bag.

Wind the strands of hair from each person together and add that to the bag.

Bind the bag shut with the blue thread.

Keep the bag in a safe place in the most used room of the house. This will drive away negative tensions and promote peace.

This spell can be refreshed monthly.

# For a Happy Home

You will need the following:

2 orange candles
Handful of lavender

Instructions:

Sprinkle the dried lavender around your altar and light the candles.

Repeat 7 times:

*This spell please bless*
*This house with happiness*

This spell can be worked weekly, with all household members present if necessary.

# To Bless a Garden

<u>You will need the following</u>:

2 cups of milk
Spoonful of honey
4 garden stakes
4 green cords
Early spring

<u>Instructions</u>:

This spell should be completed in early spring.

Mix the honey into the milk.

Outside, locate the four corners of your garden.

At each corner, pour a bit of the milk and honey, and drive and stake into the ground.

Now tie a bow around the stake and say:

*Milk and honey flowing out*
*Goddess bless my every sprout*
*Growing strong, the season's long*
*Today I bless my garden*

This spell should be repeated every spring.

# For an Abundant Garden

4 moss agate
Morning

Instructions:

Any morning, go out to your garden with the moss agate and spend a few minutes visualizing a garden teeming with flowers, vegetables, or fruits.

When ready, toss a moss agate to each of the four corners, and say:

*O bright Sun I call upon you*
*To fertilize this garden well*
*And activate the stones that fell*
*So that together you will produce*
*A wonderful garden so profuse*
*That none has ever seen its kind*
*By these words you are assigned*
*To do these things I ask of thee*
*As I will it, so mote it be*

# To Remove an Unwanted Visitor

You will need the following:

Broom

Instructions:

At any point you feel a visitor has over extended their stay, go pick up your broom and lean it against the door. No words or gestures are necessary. The visitor will quickly be ready to go.

# To Increase Luck in the Home

You will need the following:

Silver bell
White candle
Rose oil

Instructions:

In the center of your house, anoint and light the candle.

Take the bell and go to the front door.  With the door open, ring the bell 3 times while saying:

*When this bell rings my spirit sings*
*I call upon the helpful household fairies of the light*
*To bless with me magic day and night*

Go to the back door and repeat.

The candle should be allowed to finish.

# Find a Lost Object

You will need the following:

White candle

Instructions:

Light the candle and walk from room to room in the house repeating:

*I need what I seek*
*Give me a peek*
*Draw my eyes*
*To the prize*

Allow your eyes to wander around in every room. Eventually your eyes will be drawn to the area where the lost object most likely is.

# Basic Banishing

You will need the following:

Black candle
Camphor oil
Pine oil
Brown parchment & blessed pen
Fire proof dish

Instructions:

Anoint the candle with camphor oil and light it.

Write what you want to banish on the parchment, turn it sideways, and cross out what you have written 9 times.

Make a thumbprint in pine oil on the parchment.

Light the parchment, and place it in the fireproof dish to burn.

The candle should be allowed to finish. When it has done so, dispose of the ashes by flushing them down a toilet.

# Banish Depression

:

White candle
3 blue candles
Rose oil

Instructions:

While sitting down, place the white candle in front of you, the blue candles to your sides and behind you.

Light the candles.

While rubbing the rose oil on your hands, repeat 3 times:

*Anxiety, depression, emotions be,*
*I seek to cast out thee,*
*And bid you to set me free*
*From anxiety, depression, and emotions be*

Meditate for a few minutes imagining yourself totally at peace, and then snuff the candles.

# Banish Grief

<u>You will need the following</u>:

Smoky quartz
Bowl of water
3 teaspoons of salt

<u>Instructions</u>:

Hold the smoky quartz in your left hand and say:

*Banishing stone*
*Fill yourself with my grief*
*So that I may feel joy again*
*So I will it, so it be*

Add the salt to the water and stir with your right hand.

Place the smoky quartz in the water and leave the room for at least 15 minutes.

After 15 minutes, go back and get the bowl. Take the bowl outside and fling it as hard as you can away from you.

# Banish Anger

You will need the following:

Black stone
Fresh pine branches

Instructions:

Hold the black stone to your forehead. Concentrate on pushing any angry feelings from your head into the stone.

When you feel ready, take the stone and cast it into a body of water, so it is unlikely to be found by anyone.

Place pine branches at the front and back doorways of your home to prevent the anger from coming back.

# Luck Powder

<u>You will need the following</u>:

Green talc
Patchouli
Rose
Juniper berries
Dollar bill

<u>Instructions</u>:

Use equal parts talc, patchouli, rose, and juniper berries with one ground dollar bill.

This powder can be sprinkled in the doorway of your home or business, and in the corners of your home and business.

# Peace Powder

<u>You will need the following</u>:

Purple talc
Vanilla
Cinnamon
Peppermint
Patchouli

<u>Instructions</u>:

Use equal parts.

This peace powder should be rubbed onto the body to promote peace and repel negativity. Do a patch test before rubbing this all over yourself to make sure you do not have a bad reaction.

# For Good Business

You will need the following:

Green talc
Frankincense
Tonka beans

Instructions:

Use equal parts.

Burn this in a censer if you are having bad luck in business or trying to generate new business. This can be burned daily.

# Job Protection Powder

You will need the following:

Red talc
Musk
Chili powder
Tobacco

Instructions:

Use equal parts.

Discreetly sprinkle this around your work area to protect your job. This must be done in secret and can be done weekly.

# Celebration Powder

<u>You will need the following</u>:

Talc in the color of your choice
Rosemary
Cinnamon
Peppermint
Teaspoon of glitter in the color or your choice

<u>Instructions</u>:

Use equal parts except for the glitter.

Sprinkle this in your hair, or rub it on visible parts of your body for any celebratory occasion.  Do a patch test before rubbing this all over yourself to make sure you do not have a bad reaction.

# Money Powder

<u>You will need the following</u>:

Chamomile
Marigold
Hyssop
Jasmine
Cinnamon
Clove
Ginger
Nutmeg
Cinquefoil

<u>Instructions</u>:

Use equal parts.

This powder should be sprinkled anywhere you might receive money, like a mailbox.  It can be sprinkled in the four corners of your home, across your doorway, at the office, or in your purse.

# Protection Powder

You will need the following:

1 part salt
2 parts sandalwood

Instructions:

This powder should be sprinkled at the four corners of your home, outdoors. This will repel negative energy or spirits and should be refreshed monthly.

# Power Powder

You will need the following:

Silver talc
Honeysuckle
Rose
Geranium

Instructions:

Use equal parts.

This powder should be sprinkled on your ritual tools, altar, hands, written spells or books, and candles to increase the power of spells you cast.

# Dream Powder

<u>You will need the following</u>:

Light blue talc
Musk
Orris
Peppermint
Lavender

<u>Instructions</u>:

Use equal parts.

This powder can be sprinkled on your pillow, bed, under your bed, the four corners of your bedroom, or your head, before sleeping to increase your dreams.

# Success Powder

<u>You will need the following</u>:

Gold talc
Frankincense
Sandalwood
Gold glitter

<u>Instructions</u>:

Use equal parts.

This powder can be sprinkled around your altar before you begin a spell to give you a greater chance of success.

# Money Bottle

<u>You will need the following</u>:

Glass bottle
5 unsalted & unshelled peanuts
5 allspice seeds
5 cloves
5 cinnamon sticks
5 sesame seeds
5 kernels of dried corn
5 coins

<u>Instructions</u>:

Add everything to the bottle and gently shake it to combine. Say:

*Silver and spice*
*Copper and grain*
*I need to increase*
*My financial gain*

Store this bottle in the center room in your home. This bottle can be refreshed annually.

# Love Bottle

You will need the following:

Glass bottle
Rose petals
Jasmine flowers
Lavender flowers
Ginger root
Cloves
Cinnamon Stick
Red parchment & blessed pen
Red candle

Instructions:

Light the candle.

Add the rose petals, jasmine flowers, lavender flowers, ginger root, cloves, and cinnamon stick to the bottle.

On the parchment, write your name and your partner's name, and roll the paper into a tube. Drop it into the bottle and say:

*Herbs of Earth, herbs of lust*
*Bring us passion, in you I trust*

Close the bottle and seal it with wax.

This bottle should be hung from the ceiling in your bedroom. If at some point the relationship ends, the bottle should be smashed.

# Witch's Bottle

You will need the following:

Glass bottle
Dried rosemary
Dried thyme
Handful of nails
Black candle

Instructions:

Light the candle.

Fill the bottle with the rosemary, thyme, and nails.  Then say:

*In this witch's bottle of mine*
*I place nails, rosemary and thyme*
*Protect me from any enmity*
*As I will it,  so mote it be*

Allow the candle to burn for at least 10 minutes, and then seal the bottle with black wax.

The bottle should be buried at the edge of your property to destroy negativity and evil.

# Good Luck Bottle

You will need the following:

Glass bottle
Clover
Dandelion
Honeysuckle
Nutmeg
Rose hips
Tonka bean

Instructions:

Add everything to the bottle and keep it in your kitchen.  Each day, take the bottle in your hands and say:

*To God and Goddess I do pray*
*Guide me through another day*
*Let all good things come my way*
*Good luck hither, now I say*

Do this each day for a lunar cycle.  At that point, return the herbs to the Earth.  You can continue on if you like, by making a new bottle.

# Home Protection Bottle

<u>You will need the following</u>:

Glass bottle
½ cup salt
3 cloves garlic
9 bay leaves
7 teaspoons dried basil
4 teaspoons dill seeds
1 teaspoon sage
1 teaspoon black pepper
1 teaspoon white pepper
1 teaspoon fennel

<u>Instructions</u>:

Add the salt to the bottle while saying:

*Salt that protects, protect my home and all within*

Add the garlic to the bottle while saying:

*Garlic that protects, protect my home and all within*

Add the bay leaves to the bottle while saying:

*Bay that protects, protect my home and all within*

Add the basil to the bottle while saying:

*Basil that protects, protect my home and all within*

Add the dill seeds to the bottle while saying:

*Dill that protects, protect my home and all within*

Add the sage to the bottle while saying:

*Sage that protects, protect my home and all within*

Add the black and white pepper to the bottle while saying:

*Pepper that protects, protect my home and all within*

Add the fennel to the bottle while saying:

*Fennel that protects, protect my home and all within*

Close the bottle and gently shake it to combine.  Place it anywhere in your house with the words:

*Salt and herbs nine by nine*
*Now guard this home of mine*

Bottle can be refreshed annually.

# Inspiration Jar

You will need the following:

Small jar
Orange fabric
Orange ribbon or cord
2 parts dried oranges
1 part dill

Instructions:

Fill the jar with the dried oranges first, dill second.

Put the fabric over the top of jar and tie it down with the ribbon or cord.

The jar should be kept in the area where you need inspiration. The color orange increases creativity.

This jar should be refreshed weekly for as long as necessary.

# Bath to Break a Curse

You will need the following:

Black candle
Handful of white sage
Handful of lavender
Handful of chamomile
Handful of sea salt
Bathtub
Waning moon

Instructions:

Draw a warm bath.

Place the candle at the foot of the tub, and add the herbs and salt to the water.

Light the candle and let it burn at your feet while you relax in the bath.

When you are ready say:

*By the light of the moon's wane*
*Cleanse my soul of this stain*
*Let the spell be reversed*
*Lift away this dark curse*
*As I lay in my sacred space*
*Return my soul to grace*

3 times, scoop some up water, pour it over your head, and say:

*I forgive what was done*
*Let the spell be undone*

Allow the candle to finish and the spell is complete.

# Wealth Attraction Bath

<u>You will need the following</u>:

Handful of sea salt
3 drops of basil oil
3 drops of cinnamon oil
3 drops of pine oil

<u>Instructions</u>:

Draw a warm bath and add all ingredients to the water. You must soak in this bath for at least 15 minutes while visualizing yourself and your personal finances. You must visualize (no matter the true situation) that you have plenty of money to cover your current and necessary expenses.

This ritual bath can be completed weekly.

# Healing Bath

You will need the following:

White candle
Handful of sea salt
Carnation oil
Violet oil

Instructions:

Draw warm bathwater and add the sea salt and oils.

While skimming your hand over the top of the water say:

*Into this water, power I send*
*Stress shall unwind and wounds shall mend*

Light the candle and bathe only by its light.

Soak in the tub for at least 15 minutes, visualizing black sickness being drawn out of your body by the salt and oils in the water.

When you are ready, drain the tub and picture all illness flowing down the drain.

Towel dry off.

# Peace Bath

<u>You will need the following</u>:

2 cups of milk
2 tablespoons of honey
Handful of fresh mint
4 silver candles

<u>Instructions</u>:

Light a candle in each corner of the bathtub so you bathe only by candlelight.

Draw a warm bath, adding first the milk, then the honey, and last the mint.

Bathe as long as you feel necessary or until the water cools.

You may chant or pray if you feel the need to do so.

# Bath to Remove Negative Energy

You will need the following:

2 cups of vinegar
Handful of fresh rue
2 blue candles

Instructions:

Place the candles anywhere in the bathroom and draw a warm bath.

Add the vinegar and the rue to the water and stir with your hands.

Soak in the water for at least 15 minutes.

When draining the water, visualize all negative energy flowing away from you and down the drain.

# Lover's Bath

<u>You will need the following</u>:

6 oranges
Handful of rose petals
Cup of white wine
2 tablespoons of honey
6 red candles

<u>Instructions</u>:

Surround the bathtub with candles and draw a warm bath.

Add all ingredients to the water and stir with your hands.

The couple should soak in the water, in as close contact as possible, for at least 15 minutes.

# To Banish Bad Luck in Love

<u>You will need the following</u>:

Carnation oil
Time before sunrise
Bathtub
Jar

<u>Instructions</u>:

Before sunrise, fill a bath and lay back in it.

While in the water, visualize all your love troubles. Once you have done this, cast them off into the bath water.

Step out of the bath and fill your jar with bath water, draining the rest, and your bad luck troubles, down the drain.

Take the jar to the nearest crossroads and fling it towards the east.

Once back at home, anoint your hands and face with carnation oil.

# To Increase Your Romantic Energy

<u>You will need the following</u>:

2 red candles
2 pink candles
Jasmine oil

<u>Instructions</u>:

Place the 4 candles in each of the corners of the bathtub and run the water. The red candles should be where your head will be and the pink candle should be where your feet will be.

Add the jasmine oil to the water.

Remain in the bath, laid back, eyes closed, until the candles have burned down. During this time focus on being at peace in your relationship, and all the good things you have to be thankful for in your relationship.

When you are finished, drain the bath with your left hand, and air dry.

# Love Spell Chant

Repeat silently or out loud at any time:

*Star of my love, burn so bright*
*Unite my true love to me tonight*
*So I will it, so mote it be*

# Go to Sleep Chant

Repeat silently while trying to go to sleep:

*Bring me quiet*
*Bring me peace*
*Ease my dreams*
*Nightmares cease*

# Money Chant

Repeat silently or out loud at any time:

*One coin here, another coin there*
*Prosperity is everywhere*
*I need some wealth, financial health*
*Just send me my share*

# Chant for Health

Repeat silently or out loud at any time:

*Bring health to my body, and my soul too*
*Strength and well-being*
*Make it all new*

# Protection Chant

Should be repeated at least 3 times:

*Divine Goddess!*
*If evil dwells within this place*
*Please make it leave my space*

# Nighttime Protection Chant

Repeat silently or out loud at night:

*Hail fair moon*
*Ruler of the night*
*Guard me and mine*
*Until the light*

# Stress Chant

Repeat silently or out loud at any time:

*Chase this mess away*
*Keep it far from me today*

# Anxiety Chant

Repeat silently or out loud at any time:

*Nervous anxiety, you are DEAD*
*Lord and Lady, soothe my head*
*Bring me your calming peace*
*As I will it, so mote it be*

# Banish Pain Chant

Repeat silently or out loud until the pain recedes:

*Spirit of fire I call upon the immortal flame to release me of this pain*